GIRL, GET IN THE GAME!

Unlock the Secrets of Gamification to Grow Your Business

Sandra D. Cleveland, Ph.D., RN

For information on bulk orders or to have Sandra D. Cleveland speak at your event, please contact Sandra D. Cleveland at: tribeconsulting4u@gmail.com

Library of Congress Cataloging – in-Publication Data has been applied for.

Publishing Services By: Pen Legacy LLC (www.penlegacy.com)
Cover Design By: Tamika Ink
Edited By: Heather Asiyanbi
Formatting By: Carla M. Dean, U Can Mark My Word

Paperback ISBN: 979-8-9868377-4-1

PRINTED IN THE UNITED STATES OF AMERICA.

FIRST EDITION

Table of Content

DEDICATION

*I dedicate this to all of the wonderful Women CEOs
who have a servant spirit and strive to maintain a sense of fun in life,
but who are ready to make a change to reach their dreams
and expand their business – this one's for you.*

GIRL, GET IN THE GAME!

Unlock the Secrets of Gamification to Grow Your Business

INTRODUCTION

I f you are a solopreneur struggling with things like marketing to your target client or developing learning for employees that keeps them engaged, then this book is meant for you! Cause here's the thing, ladies: We have this superpower in our tool belt, but we need to wrangle this superpower in the way that is meant for US.

How do we harness the power of gamification to show off our creativity, our vibe, and our business without always using the standard blueprint? We're going to talk about how to infuse gamification strategies into your customers' and employees' experiences that speak to your business branding and mission.

I'll share some of the science of gamification in entrepreneurship. We'll look at existing industry knowledge, thoughts on gamification, and the art of gamification in entrepreneurship. I provide a framework that incorporates internal and external factors, such as creativity, needed to build your distinctive game plan. The use of gamification can help you stand out from the crowd and bring your unique flavor.

Let me spill some tea, though. Gamifying our businesses won't work unless we let our creativity lead the way. Let me spill a little more tea: You are a creative being. No matter what you've been told before or believe about yourself, you already have or can build creativity. Every time you work to refine a process or implement a new idea in your business, you are using creativity to experiment and play.

You may be thinking, "But I'm not a gamer." You don't need to be! Gamification goes beyond just playing a video game when you use it in a way that's playful and purposeful for you and your intended audience. It doesn't matter if the goal of an action you take is to invite, incite, ignite, or inform your intended audience. You'll be guided in developing bespoke action plans customized that equip you, steering your business toward innovation.

CHAPTER 1
GAMIFICATION IS A GAME CHANGER

Hey, to all my new Girl Boss friends! I'm so glad you decided to embark on this journey with me to understand gamification and how to use it as a superpower in your business. Gamification, when used effectively, can help us amplify our business branding, processes, and voice. Let's face it, ladies. We need this in a world that sometimes works to silence us.

I need you to hear me – really hear me – when I say: *Do NOT let the mindset of the world create your narrative.* You are the author of your story, and part of your story revolves around the business you birthed. You know that voice in your head that tells you to doubt yourself? I named my voice Sheneneh (Shah-nay-nay) after the character in 90's TV show, *Martin.* When Sheneneh speaks, she can sometimes be my worst critic because she represents the naysayers and haters who work to knock me down. Here's the thing, Boo, those naysayers and haters are NOT part of my target audience so what they say is none of my business. Did you *feel* me when I said that? Let me repeat it for those in the back: What others say about you is NONE OF YOUR BUSINESS.

Gamification is a concept that is becoming part of business culture. Let's look at a couple of stats about the use of gamification:

- 70% of global 2000 companies surveyed use gamification in some way.
- According to Zippia.com, 95% of employees said they enjoyed aspects of gamification at work (yes, girl, 95%!).
- Business leaders are gaming, too. According to PopCap games, 40% of more than 7,000 execs surveyed are playing games during work.
- 50% of start-ups use gamification.

Ladies, here's what I need you to understand about the data. The data does not state that 70% of male-run businesses use gamification or that 95% of employees who enjoy aspects of gamification at work are all male. Women enjoy games as well! Think about your target customer and their characteristics, not just their behaviors. I bet good money I don't have (yet) that most of you target women. Who better to speak about your products and services using gamification in a way that is engaging and specific to this audience? You, you, and you.

Girl, it behooves you to improve processes and efficiencies in your business for your employees and your customers. Gamification, when used properly, can positively impact both the employee and customer experiences by making them something they remember and want to repeat. The result can be greater employee productivity, increased customer engagement, and, ultimately, a boost for your bottom line. Are you pumped? Good! Let us get this party started by defining gamification and how it can change the trajectory of your business.

What is Gamification?

In 2002, computer programmer Nick Pelling coined the term *gamification*, which originally described using game-like accelerated user interface design to improve the speed and enjoyment of electronic transactions. Anyone besides me struggle with this definition? It's the idea of using game mechanics (i.e., the parts that make a game) to nudge our behavior, providing purpose and meaning. A quick example is the Greenlight app, a debit card and budgeting app for teens. Financial incentives are built into the app encouraging its users to save more. Using things such as incentives, rewards, and our ingrained need to play, gamification is injected into our real-life applications such as fitness and education.

Today, there is no one accepted definition of the term. However, the core meaning of gamification involves digitally using experience design and game mechanics to engage and motivate people to achieve their goals. The term *experience design* is used to describe the journey game players take; this design contains features like gameplay (the actual interaction with the game), play space, and storyline. *Game mechanics or game elements* describe the major features in many games, like points, badges, and leaderboards. So, with gamification, the player is *digitally engaging* rather than personally engaging. This means that users are interacting with smartphones, smartwatches, computers, or other digital devices. The purpose of gamification is to motivate people by driving innovation, developing skills, or changing behaviors. Gamification has an impact on your body's physical response to the activity as well by releasing dopamine, considered the "feel-good" hormone. By permitting users to achieve their goals, workplace organizations can realize their objectives. Admit it. You read this definition and thought, "Blah, blah, blah." Yeah, me, too. Let's break this definition down a little more.

Gamification is not creating a video game. It is using key gaming features like game mechanics, design techniques, and certain behavioral elements in an environment we don't normally use them, specifically, in non-gaming situations. Gamification entails using important game elements that typically engage users, such as competition, visible achievements, and design, and applying them to non-game things. For instance, gamification can be used when working on a task, learning, or purchasing goods and services. The aspects of game mechanics commonly used when things are gamified include leaderboards, badges, and points. You see gamification used in areas such as education and business. You see it used in social media. Why use it in areas such as these? Gamification used as part of your strategy allows you to ante up the ways you engage, educate, excite, or evaluate your customers or employees. In simpler terms, gamification makes productivity game-like. It's about using the *art* of game design to positively affect real-world productivity. Games are designed to please the humans playing them. Games also come with objectives, like saving a princess or slaying the dragon. These objectives keep players engaged and committed to the game as they enjoy compelling, playful experiences. Via gamification, game mechanics and techniques can be combined to form engaging and joyful experiences for everyone.

Gamification is not just about building games for business uses. It involves increasing the operation of an already-prevailing process or experience in your business, instead of creating something new from the ground up. Ladies, what this means is that adding gamified components won't resolve a jacked-up process. An estimated 80% of workplace gamification efforts fail to fully meet a company's objectives due to poor planning and design as well as a lack of creativity and meaning. The failure rate does not mean that gamification doesn't work for those companies. The intent to incorporate gamification strategies is present, but there can be a lack of due diligence. As a result, it means that the companies experienced success but not at the rate they anticipated. Don't think you are a gamer or being influenced by gamification? Think again.

A Partial Day in the Life of the Gamified Girl Boss

Let's look at how gamification plays a part in the details of your life in ways that have become second nature:

- You wake up and decide to meditate using an app with an annual subscription where you can monitor your daily progress (streaks) and receive immediate, positive feedback when you complete a meditation session.

- You have a plane to catch, so you check the airline's app and congratulate yourself for collecting and using frequent flier miles so this trip is free. (Yeah, I know that you could write this off if this was a business trip, but this is imaginary.)

- Your kids are on their way home from school. You use an app on your way to the airport to remind them about their chores that also records when they successfully complete them and how much they earned for each one. Your children can watch their money grow and better understand saving for their goals.

- While waiting for your flight, you participate in the airport's recognition of Heart Health Month by playing an interactive game. You learn basic first aid techniques and earn badges for your progress.

- After you land, the airline sends a survey via email. This isn't a normal survey. Rather, it's organized in a series of "Would You Rather" questions giving you two choices with picture representations of options A and B.

- You arrange transportation from the airport with a car-share service. You track your driver on a screen that depicts a car avatar on the screen moving toward your location. After you arrive at your destination, you send a tip to the driver and leave a review for them.

Your imaginary day in-the-life contains a few examples of how gamification is incorporated into your day, but let's look at how gamification examples helped the businesses:

- By including rewards like badges and positive messaging, the meditation app inspires you to keep going by matching an external incentive with the internal feelings of greater well-being. Because the meditation app subscription is renewed automatically using the credit card you paid with during your initial registration, the app generates revenue using an out-of-sight-out-of-mind model.
- The airline understands that your time is your money, and they want to make your reward membership with them as easy to navigate as possible. By putting all the features most important to you in their app, the airline lets you know that it values your time and your business so you keep flying with them.
- The airport builds community connections and potentially increases the safety of all passengers and personnel by teaching people like you how to deliver first aid in a safe learning environment
- The car-share service keeps you engaged by delivering a great customer experience through the app. Not only can you see exactly where your driver is, the service makes it easy for you to reward your driver. When you combine the two, the service increases the likelihood that you'll use them again and tell your family and friends to use them as well.

- The marketing teams of the meditation app, the airline, the airport, and the car-sharing service track user metrics through their apps to design even better experiences to keep you coming back.

See what I'm getting at? Gamifying certain aspects of your customer's or employee's experience with your business makes sense, plus dollars and cents! Despite how quickly it feels like technology is out of date, gamification isn't going anywhere.

The Two Sides of the Gamification Coin – Art and Science

There's an *art* and a *science* to gamification. The art of gamification allows you to creatively develop a game layer on top of the real business world. The science of gamification is based on the study and the use of studied concepts. Both of them need to be addressed so that you get a more well-rounded picture about the need to gamify your business.

The Art of Gamification – The Importance of Gaming Elements

Gamification involves applying game-playing elements to non-game activities. Common gaming elements are leaderboards, badges, timers, and points, which are crucial to learning and engagement. It doesn't mean making workplace activities look like a videogame. Let's talk about why some of these gaming elements are so important to elevate the engagement of your team.

1. **Progression (Achievement):** Examples of progression include badges, certificates, leaderboards, leveling, points, and progression bars. By utilizing these metrics, you can give your team dopamine hits for developing their skills and leveling up their expertise. The recognition they receive can be small, but it's powerful. In this way, they experience a sense of progression that encourages sustained effort. Leaderboards, badges, and points also deliver a social status element to the user. The brain naturally wants to experience growth and feel progress, and your workers experience these emotions when using badges and levels to visualize progress.

2. **Rewards:** Power-ups, bonuses, and collectibles. Rewards can be programmed into the total experience to provide actual sources of satisfaction for the user. Rewards delivered after a few actions are performed provides extrinsic recognition and motivation for enhancing skills, putting in effort, or recording a certain amount of time toward an objective.

3. **Story:** People are more motivated to perform tasks when it is linked to a compelling story or beating the competition as part of a narrative, like a quest-and-narrative arc. Characters, conflicts, and resolutions help immerse the players into the storyline and keep them working toward the goal.

4. **Time:** Examples of time elements include schedule and countdown. Employing time as a game element creates a sense of urgency, and helps the user schedule events and

arrange tasks and encourages greater focus on the task at hand as well.

5. **Personalization:** Interactive conversation, character naming, avatar selection, and avatar customization give users a certain identity within the game. When a person can resonate with an on-screen character or avatar, it enhances motivation and engagement.

6. **Micro interactions:** Examples of micro interactions include toggles, special effects, Easter eggs, and animated rollovers, details that create a more authentic and engaging experience[1]. Games that offer satisfying moments through micro interactions are more immersive and compelling. With cool transitions, subtle animations, and sound, the player stays engaged and more easily achieves the desired objectives.

"She Blinded Me with Science!" – The Science Behind the Magic of Gamification

If we understand what your potential customers are thinking and feeling when they interact with your business, you can provide opportunities for them to engage more, which means more customers and more money for you! So, find your inner Katherine Johnson or Bill Nye (or whoever you name your inner scientist), and let's talk a little bit about the science found in gamification. But before we begin, I want to share a story. It's not my story – it's the story of Elle Woods. Remember her? She was

---

[1] Easter eggs are hidden elements players access through certain combinations of buttons, "secret" passwords, remote areas of the game, and more.

the protagonist in the movie, *Legally Blonde,* back in the day. "It was a fun movie, but I want to focus on Elle's motivation. When we talk about Elle, one of the things we note is how her character develops throughout the film. When we see her initially, she is motivated by her peers, their sorority, and honoring the pledges they made to each other.

When she decided to go to law school, she was motivated by a combination of revenge and a need to prove herself to her boyfriend/ex-boyfriend. She encountered professors and fellow students who didn't believe she fit the accepted narrative of what a lawyer should look and sound like. At the beginning of the movie, Elle felt certain she could contribute to the field but wasn't sure how. By the end of the film, though, Elle found motivators that allowed her to discover who she really is and become a lawyer with a specific viewpoint. Bear with me. I promise this story has a point.

Like us, Elle needed motivation to move forward. There are two types of motivation—intrinsic and extrinsic. Intrinsic meant Elle had inside of her what she needed to do to move forward. Because *Legally Blonde* is a movie, we get to hear her thoughts through applicable dialogue. She stated both what she was going to do plus the reasons she was taking those actions. In this way, Elle shared her intrinsic motivators. She wanted to show and prove to her boyfriend, to the professors and fellow students, and to herself that she could graduate from law school.

Elle also had extrinsic motivating factors, like making her own money. Lawyers make good money, and money can be a powerful extrinsic motivator. In short, an extrinsic motivation originates from outside of ourselves. How the heck does Elle's story come into play with what I'm talking about?

Gamification is Largely About Motivation

Let's say you need a new dress, and you use your favorite retailer's app to find the perfect outfit. After you find a few options and add them to your cart, you see a countdown timer at the top of the page and a note in red on a couple of items letting you know there are limited quantities available. Both urge you to purchase quickly, introducing a sense of FOMO (fear of missing out). Once you make the purchase and receive your confirmation email, you feel like you won, and you got a great deal. That's enough to put a smile on your face for a few hours. The timer and the inventory notice are both extrinsic motivators, but in a way, both introduce a level of competition, too. You're in a race against time and other shoppers who may want to buy the same items. The app is built to keep you involved. Motivation and competition are both components of gamification and are both part of the science of it as well.

When I talk about the science of gamification, I mean both your physiology and your psychology. Gamification not only plays with your body but also with your mind. Let's dive into both.

The Physiology of Gamification

Games have a biological effect on learning. Playing games releases dopamine and serotonin, the happiness hormones, both of which have positive effects on both our memory and our ability to understand complex subjects faster. A well-known book from

Kapp in 2012 shared that both happiness hormones help people be more creative and better at problem-solving. These hormones also tend to make people more creative and better at problem-solving. Gamification serves as a way to access these powerful cognitive hormones through a more relaxed and fun learning environment.

The Psychology of Gamification and Game-Based Learning

Psychology plays a crucial role in activities that require motivation, behavioral patterns, and thought. Of course, gamification is deeply rooted in these psychological principles, bringing about emotions that lead to a positive user experience. Let's go over some of the reasons why gamification is so powerful.

1. **Control:** Every business understands the value of driving potential customers toward its desired goal. Yet, psychologically, human beings are not inclined to be dragged or forced to a destination. People prefer to be the masters of their own destiny because we have an instinctive need to feel in control. Gamification puts users in the driver's seat, allowing them to make their own decisions. Motivation is a key element in every gamified system. People feel more motivated to complete a task or accomplish a goal when they are in charge, or simply when they believe they are in charge. Even the perception of control drives people to chase a goal and energizes them to complete the task.

2. **Direction and Progress:** People want to understand

where they are going and to see how much progress they are making in the process. Gamification is a way to keep users in the know and offers them feedback about how far they have left to go before reaching a goal. For instance, employing gaming elements like milestones of achievement or a visual progress bar breaks down the journey into segments and makes the path toward objectives seem more manageable.

3. **Reinforces Good Behavior:** Humans love to be rewarded for their hard work. A gamified system rewards users when they do something positive. When they complete a level, a reward reinforces that behavior or habit. People love rewards because it connects them to a sense of achievement. Regardless of how big or small a milestone is, recognizing it drives action by providing a sense of accomplishment. Through a gamified system, workplaces encourage their employees to improve their skills and complete additional training. Organizations also use gamification to enhance the positive behaviors of employees and encourage them to accomplish otherwise boring tasks they would otherwise push to the side. Gamification works with the human brain, creating a natural reward compulsion loop. When you perform an action and earn a reward, it triggers a dopamine hit. This is the "feel-good" neurotransmitter we recognize as excitement that makes us repeat the action, hoping for the same result or an even better one. When you reward your employees, you create a compulsion loop that keeps

employees on task and alert. Our brains are wired to repeat actions that provide pleasure, which is why positive feedback is so effective.

4. **A Sense of Achievement:** Achievement is a powerful psychological element of human behavior. Everything people do is geared toward achieving something. Gamification allows users to break down their goals into milestones for multiple opportunities to experience that sense of achievement. For example, you can assign point values to specific work activities. You've immediately created an environment where titles, ranks, or levels matter and have the potential to evoke a sense of achievement. By creating more ways for people to feel that sense of fulfillment, you also enhance competence. The more time people spend on an activity, the better they get at it; and the more competent a person feels, the more likely they will be to continue doing that activity. Additionally, researchers have also found that effort creates excellence and can motivate people to continue learning.

5. **Goal Setting and Competition:** Human nature has evolved so we are psychologically competitive and naturally compelled to push further and harder. In that same spirit, human beings have a desire to compete with each other. That is what has gotten us to the point where we are today in our culture. One person achieves something, but there is always another person there to figure out how to do it better or faster. When people think

another team member might be outpacing them, they perceive more value in a task, which motivates them to complete it.

6. **Exploration and Escapism**: Escapism is a very unique factor available through games. There is a lot that we do in a day that is mundane and boring. Gamification offers users the freedom to explore make-believe environments and manufactures new ways to engage. By allowing users to explore these new worlds, they re-engage with something that may have become commonplace. This generates positive user experiences, increases engagement, and fuels loyalty.

7. **Exclusivity:** Leadership boards and scores in gamified systems create a space for exclusivity. Exclusivity creates curiosity, competition, and intrigue. Progress provides a dopamine hit, driving the user to remain engaged.

8. **Teamwork:** Another important psychological component of gamification is the sense of collaboration and community it offers. As social animals, people love to feel like part of a community or team on a bigger, more significant journey. Gamification can easily accomplish this, and can create loyalty and positive user experiences in the process. When the goal is finally reached and success is achieved, that conquest belongs to the group and can be shared collectively. The reward system is crucial in gamification. In the workplace, employees become more willing to share their work and collaborate when they are rewarded for doing so.

A Quick Note

You do NOT want to tackle everything in your business at once. You need to prioritize your business goals to avoid feeling overwhelmed and end up in paralysis analysis (i.e., you freeze up and don't take action on anything).

ADDING GAMIFICATION TO YOUR BUSINESS STRATEGIES IS SOMETHING *EVERY* WOMAN CEO CAN DO.

CHAPTER 2
GAMIPHI THEORY IN ACTION

G irl Boss, the struggle was real in writing this book. I am an overthinker. When I was writing this book, I kept adding a lot of information about gamification to make sure you understand the concept. At the same time, I realized that including a bunch of disconnected information wouldn't make this book useful. I wanted to explain the thoughts in my head so they made sense, to incorporate issues currently affecting business, and to level the business playing field for US. Finally, I wanted to keep it REAL. This is how my framework, The GamiPHI Theory, was born. Before I describe the GamiPHI Theory, please understand that the term, "theory," is not used in the scientific meaning of the word. Instead, I use it to refer to a group of underlying principles that lead us toward creative connection. Before jumping into The GamiPHI Theory, I want to address the concept of creativity. It is such an important idea to help us get in the game.

Sandra Cleveland, Ph.D., RN

What is Creativity?

Creativity is an intrinsic concept that nearly everyone finds hard to define. We can relate with creative people and the results of their creativity: Steve Jobs, the creator of Apple, Bill Gates, the creator of Microsoft, Frida Kahlo, a famous painter, and Thomas Edison, the inventor of the light bulb. However, coming up with a definition that captures the concept entirely is difficult. I love the definitions shared by Ava Duvernay and Albert Einstein:

"Creativity is an energy. It's a precious energy, and it's something to be protected. A lot of people take for granted that they're a creative person, but I know from experience, feeling it within myself, it is a magic; it is an energy, and it can't be taken for granted."

~ Ava Duvernay

"Creativity is intelligence Having Fun"

~ Albert Einstein

Don't you just love these definitions? They both speak volumes to me. Creativity is something we need to nurture in our businesses. Two assumptions that I made when writing this book were that both organizations and individuals want to be creative. Let's understand their definitions because you will nurture both.

Organizational creativity was first defined by Teresa Amabile in 1983 as the making of a prize and useful new product, service, idea, or process by a group of individuals working together to achieve a common goal in a complex social system. Organizational creativity is only valuable if implemented and adapted into the culture, ethics, values, structure, and processes of the organization. In 2008, Amabile partnered with Mukti Khaire to define *individual creativity* as the use of a person's mind to generate something unique and original that is useful for people beyond the originator of the ideas. Every individual has the potential for creative abilities in the form of expertise (i.e., the knowledge an individual possesses that can be applied to his or her work in order to improve output), creative thinking (i.e., the capacity to judiciously garner the existing ideas and put them together in new combinations), and motivations (i.e., the need and passion for an individual to be creative).

My GamiPHI Theory aims to explain the factors underpinning a healthy, creative organizational culture. It identifies how an employee's perception of the organizational culture and practices impacts their willingness to engage creatively. You should know the importance of how the employee perceives the work environment aligns with the organizational view, meaning it takes both your workers and the structure you've built in your business to create opportunities where gamification and play strategies support innovation.

The GamiPHI theory is derived from a number of theories from various fields. For instance, Pender's Health Promotion Model is noted. The basis for this model notes how a person's health behavior is influenced by different factors and helps identify when interventions from health component organizations might take place. Education learning theories were also considered as we need to understand the needs and perceptions of employees.

The GamiPHI Theory incorporates behavioral psychology concepts, as these largely speak to the ideas of engagement and motivation. Organizational culture framework also contributed to GamiPHI theory with its focus on alignment and the concepts of incorporating gaming for purpose and play. Therefore, the gamification theory and the play theory are included as well.

Introducing the GamiPHI Theory

The GamiPHI Theory contains three major components, or pillars:

- Play Potential
- Health Perception
- Innovation Potential

The following image is a schematic representation of the GamiPHI theory.

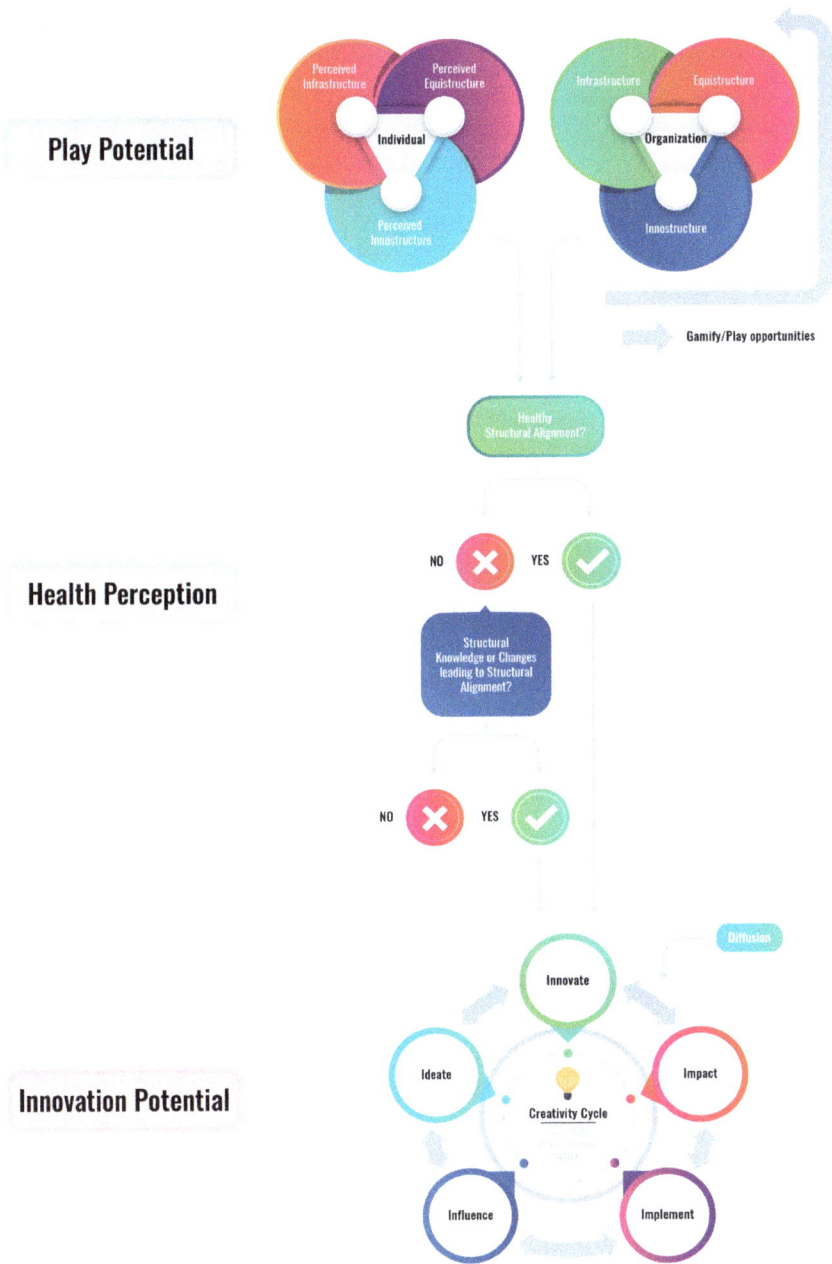

Figure 1. The GamiPHI Theory

Sandra Cleveland, Ph.D., RN

When discussing the GamiPHI theory, the primary differentiator from previously discussed theories is the incorporation of play and gamification. Play, health, and innovation are where the PHI in the term GamiPHI is incorporated.

Pillar One: Play Potential

In the first pillar, there are basically two perspectives: that of the individual and that of the organization. When we talk about play potential, think about the written and unwritten rules of the playground. It's important to note both the individual (i.e., the players) and the organization perspective (i.e., parents, teachers, monitors). Within the play potential component, there are three similar *structures* from the individual and the organization's perspective; Infrastructure, and I have coined Equistructure, and Innostructure (see Figure 2).

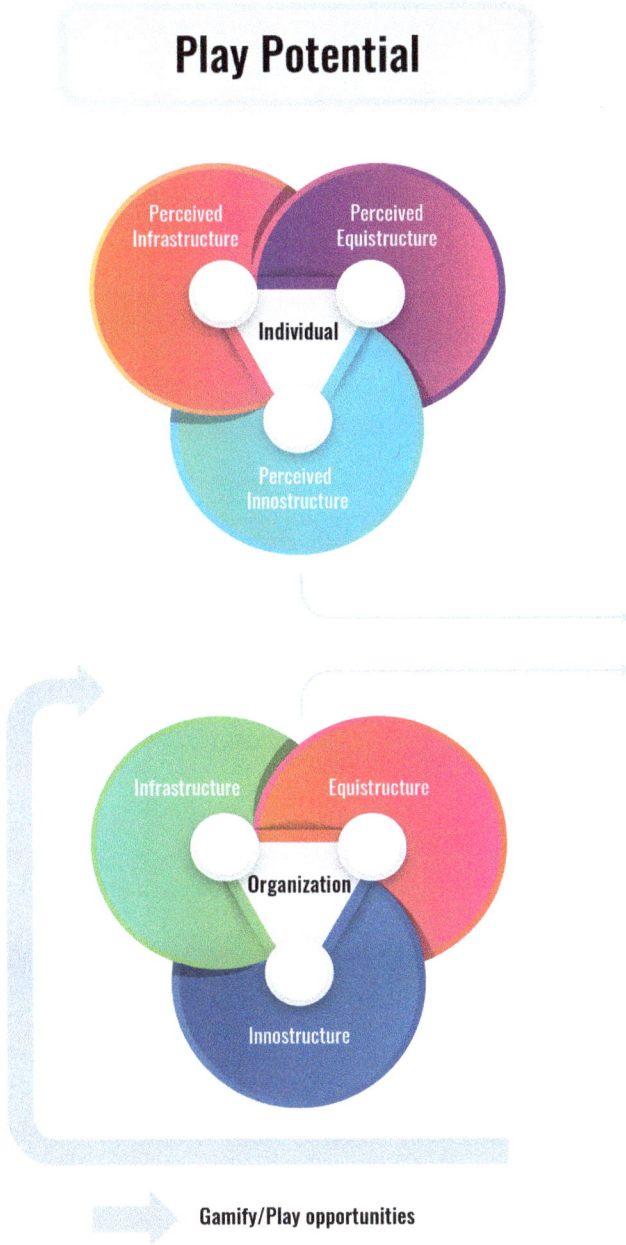

Play Potential

Perceived Infrastructure

Perceived Equistructure

Individual

Perceived Innostructure

Infrastructure

Equistructure

Organization

Innostructure

Gamify/Play opportunities

Figure 2. The Play Potential Pillar of The GamiPHI Theory

- *Infrastructure* consists of anything process-related; or, resources from the organization's perspective. Specifically, leveraging process, system processes, risks, and rewards.
- *Equistructure* is the diversity, equity, and inclusion factor organizations understand are necessary for every member of your team to see creative opportunities. Empowerment and psychological safety are important components of the equistructure pillar.
- *Innostructure,* the process used to move creatively towards innovation. Many organizations strive for innovation but don't always get there. GamiPHI theory contends that creativity is a prerequisite to innovation and needs to be honed. Organizational leaders—and if you are the sole leader, this is especially true—affect the 5-I process (coming soon), and have to demonstrate their commitment to innovative practice and rewarding employee innovation.

But the focus is not just on the organization; the perception of each employee about their potential for creativity is included. Remember, you can't have one without the other. Using the words, "perceived," and "perception," is intentional because organizations may say they have available resources, but individuals may perceive those tools as unavailable to them based on their position or whatever factors (or vice versa). It's important to note both the individual and organization standpoints in terms of play potential, both of which factor into the health perception.

How Do We Gamify the Play Potential Pillar?

Remember, the Play Potential is focused on the three structure types: innostructure, equistructure, and infostructure. The common goal for each of these structures is for the employee to learn about and employ processes and relationships that have meaning for them and helps the organization meet the KPIs. A caveat about using gamification in this pillar: While gamifying common work experiences can be fun, the primary point is to move employees toward the behaviors needed to reach the goals. This is what makes you a different type of CEO. You work to provide experiences without diminishing the necessary conversations. You could gamify identifying the process issues in moving a customer along the customer journey in your app or on your website. As customers complete tasks—missions—they receive rewards. Your marketing team can track customers who move from consideration to conversation to acting as an ambassador by sharing a review or taking a survey. The more complicated the task, the higher the award associated with it.

Pillar Two: Health Perception

Health is a big component that needs attention in our businesses. The health and wellness of an organization is just as important as the health and wellness of the individuals who are within the organization. Remember, in the Play Potential pillar, that the individual reviews the three structures (equistructure, infrastructure, and innostructure) to see if their perception of these structures align with how the organization has positioned them. The individual then decides if the differences noted between the

Sandra Cleveland, Ph.D., RN

organization's structure and her perception of the organization's structure is something she can deal with or not, i.e. determining the health of the organization. This decision falls within the Health Perception Pillar, the second pillar of the GamiPHI Theory as represented in Figure 3.

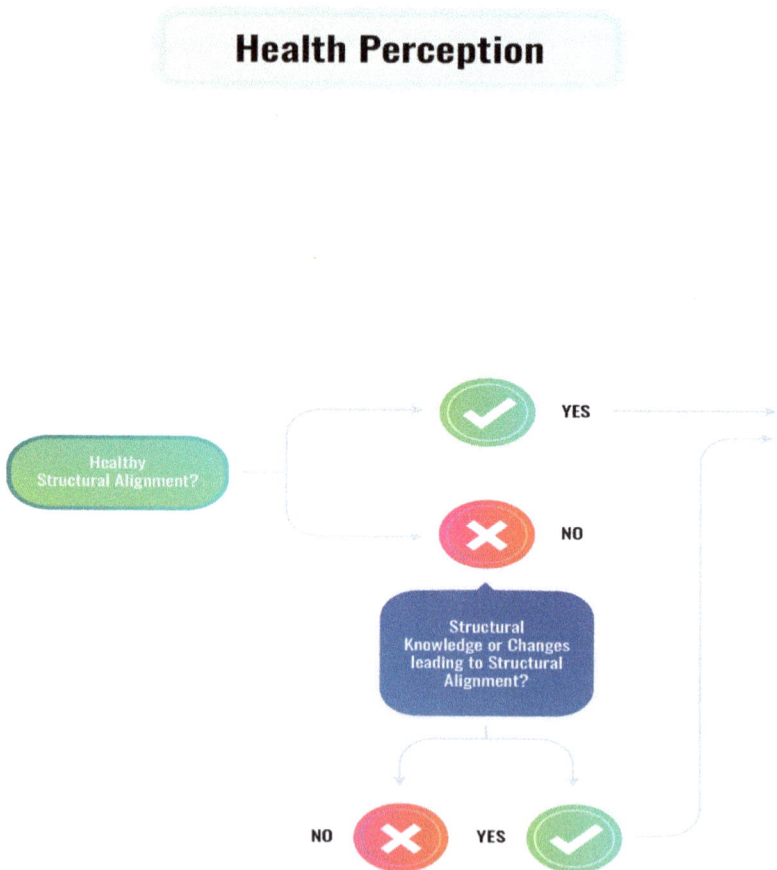

Health Perception

Healthy Structural Alignment?

YES

NO

Structural Knowledge or Changes leading to Structural Alignment?

NO   YES

Figure 3. The Health Perception Pillar of The GamiPHI Theory

38

If there is healthy structural alignment, you will see that it goes across into the Innovation Potential pillar. This is good because it means your employee is willing to share their creative gifts with you. On the other hand, if your employee feels a misalignment between their perception and the organization's understanding of an issue, that person may choose to temporarily disengage. As the business owner, you need to identify where the necessary change should occur.

Our goal here is to re-engage the person, so the feedback loop brings us back to the Play Potential to make adjustments to the structures. For instance, your employee may need to learn more about your benefits package because they did not realize that it was already available to them. Or maybe from the organization standpoint (that's you), you think your current equistructure offerings as fair and equitable— but what you deliver may not align with the employee's experience, making you rethink and adjust policy or practice.

May I spill some tea here, ladies? Please listen when your employees share their concerns with you! They are still at the stage where they are willing to remain engaged with you and the business. If your organization has a healthy structural alignment, gamification can be used proactively to continue building on what has been working for you. If your organization is perceived as having some fissures in the alignment, there are opportunities to rebuild using gamification strategies.

Note: if a person stays stuck in the feedback loop, they may then choose (or the organization may identify) their lack of fit and move from disengagement to attrition. But if your employee

39

perceives that structural alignment is intact, then we move forward to the third pillar, Innovation Potential.

How Do We Gamify the Health Perception Pillar?

Have you ever reached out to your team to get their take on the work culture? And the only response was the sound of crickets? This is a common struggle for many women CEOs. Employees may want to share their honest opinions but are worried that they will go unheard or be retaliated against. Hear me when I say this: The opinions they hold about the business will influence their behaviors at work. The key to this stage is your employees' perceptions, and they may not always be willing to share them with you. The Health Perception Pillar is focused on the employee's perception of her own health and the health of your small business. You can incorporate gamification into the sharing opinions.

How do you do this? You pose questions around the concepts of work culture, business health, and employee health using the game of "Would You Rather," a party game that poses a dilemma in the form of a question that starts with the words, "Would you rather". There are two ways you might incorporate this; by posing a series of questions online and gathering the data for the group or by holding in-person or remote sessions so workers get to know one another better, which has a direct result on your employees' health. Here's how an in-person or live remote game would work:

Let the employees self-separate into teams if you're in person or place your workers in randomly selected breakout rooms if you're remote and tell them they're playing for a certain number of points. One person serves as the respondent and writes down their answers to a series of three to five questions. One person is the designated host who reads each question out loud. Each additional player guesses what the respondent answered, who then reveals correct and incorrect answers. If no one guesses the employee's answers, then the respondent earns three points. If someone guesses correctly, they earn one point. Continue going around the group until the winner is declared (i.e., whoever gets the identified number of points wins). Make sure to identify the goal—the KPI—you are trying to achieve when implementing the game. Key performance indicators are what you use to make sure you're meeting your goals both in the short and the long term. If the KPI is focused on more employee interaction, option two might work best. If the KPI is focused on gathering the pulse of your employees' thoughts on the current state of the work culture, your business' health and their own health, consider option one. Most importantly, close the feedback loop! Share what findings came out of the data and see if it rings true from the employees' perspectives.

Pillar Three: Innovation Potential

This pillar in the GamiPHI Theory moves your worker(s) forward; from their willingness and perceived ability to be creative to the process of actually being creative both independently and collaboratively. The five parts of the process are deemed the "5-I" creativity cycle: ideate, influence, implement, impact, and innovate. Think of the cycle as a flywheel that produces its own momentum. And even though employees will

41

Sandra Cleveland, Ph.D., RN

repeat the cycle, movement might not always be linear. They might move back and forth based on feedback they get (note Figure 4).

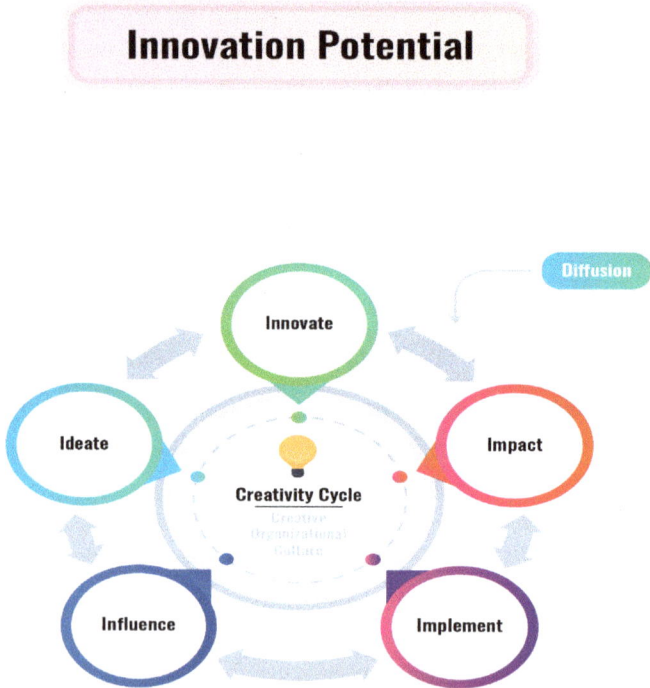

Figure 4. The Innovation Potential Pillar of The GamiPHI Theory

Ideate is the first stage of the creativity cycle, brainstorming the idea. Next, the idea needs leadership buy-in, the influence, to move the idea forward into action. Once they have the influence they need, they can work toward an implementation plan that includes measuring impact. Typically, those are the four stages of the creativity cycle that most people go through. It does not matter what level of employee is going through this process. It may be an idea related to their particular role, their department, or the organization. The last step is the biggest, but it makes all the difference between what is a creative concept and what is innovation. I refer to the concept of diffusion.

Ladies, think about the opportunities you might have to diffuse ideas through your business. For instance, can we try an idea, refine it and attempt the revised version first in the same way but also apply it to another aspect of our business?

Questions we might ask to determine if innovation is occurring in your small business:

- Can we move the idea from the unit level to the department level?
- Does it diffuse through other areas in your business?
- Are you considered a thought leader in your industry?

Let's take an example. Social media has increasingly become a method of communication with potential clients, to share your business' vision, mission, and values, and to help link these to potential clients' stories as well. During your staff meetings, the marketing department reported that they created lists of relevant keywords and phrases for the website. The data shows the bounce rate, i.e. the time potential clients leave the website, has decreased dramatically and they met this KPI. As a result of this conversation, the customer service department wants to take the process used in marketing to update the activity on the customer community website.

Diffusion is the difference between moving ideas forward from creative ideas that impact the initially designed area to actual initial groundwork for innovation.

How Do We Gamify the Innovation Potential Pillar?

Remember the days of the suggestion box? This was often the way employees were tapped for new ideas to mixed results. The other common idea was a dedicated "think tank" consisting of a few individuals from the business to generate ideas. While this may have helped generate ideas, buy-in from other employees was mixed. What were these ideas missing? Incentivization and community. But even these two ideas present challenges when used. If the right incentives as perceived by your employees are not in place, they are apt to not engage. Additionally, if the employee feels forced to work in a group, you most likely won't see the best results. Enter gamification. Remember the social media success of the marketing department in the earlier example? You could hold an "Innovation Blitz" month. Teams would use collective wisdom to incorporate social media strategies in their respective departments. You award points to teams that onboard the quickest into the challenge, and your customers upvote the social media idea from each department they like best. The winners receive a badge and an announcement on the company's social media channels. The game doesn't need to stop here – it can continue with the implementation of the ideas to see who best meets the KPI with the prize being a social media campaign dedicated to their success.

Conclusion

Alright, Girl Boss. Remember when I stated early in the book that we can bring our unique superpowers to the table when incorporating gamification? This chapter on the GamiPHI Theory provides ways that you can identify the perceptions made by your employees and move proactively to address those concerns.

Here are some takeaways:

- We need to address the infrastructure, equistructure (i.e., equity practices), and innostructure (i.e., innovation practices) built into our organizational culture.
- The way an organization makes the effort to play, stay healthy, and innovate are vital to both the employees and organization.
- Your employees may make a cognitive decision to mentally and/or physically disconnect from your business because they perceive misalignment between their views and your views.
- You can use gamification to address perceived misalignment or fissures in the structures.

Girl, do you understand the value given here? Do you see the possibilities to develop your gamified programs that can make you a thought leader in your industry? The bottom line: -- there are a number of variables we need to pay attention to, the biggest of which is your employee's perception of your business.

Listen, Girl Boss – are you ready?! It's game-time.

We've spent time learning the concept of gamification and understanding the framework to help make your gamified offerings unique to the needs of your business. The final chapter is moving from thoughts to ACTION (I mean, that's what you came here for, right?). I'm going to talk about the customer and employee journey – what are the stages for each with examples of gamification thrown in. Then I have thrown in some common business situations that have been gamiPHI-ed. Last, I'll share one additional situation that we'll work through together to formulate potential metrics and a way to gamiPHI the process. Let's go!

P.S. If you are that person who wants to dive more into the full explanation of The GamiPHI Theory, my book, *The Play-Based Organization,* contains The GamiPHI Theory in its totality.

CHAPTER 3
GAMIFICATION IN ACTION

I absolutely appreciate that you've stuck with me this far. At the beginning of this book, I promised that I would share examples of how you can use gamification in your small business, and I'm here to deliver the goods. Did you know that in the video games currently available that male characters are four times more common than female characters? UGH! I know! Females are more sexualized in the game and often subordinate to male characters. But remember, I wrote this book so we can change the game. As the HWIC (head woman in charge), you get to create a plot twist to the typical game narratives for your business! Gamification allows us to create stories that reflect OUR world. Gamifying your business processes can help you move forward in the roles that mean a lot to you. Based on the purpose of the project in which you incorporate gamification, you become an advocate, an activist, an educator, a health/wellness coach, a strategist, and more. First, look at all the players who have an experience – i.e., your customers and your employees. Both of these groups experience a journey from the point of their first encounter with your business until a separation from your business is taken.

Gamification is about the individual FIRST.

When you play games, there is an end goal in mind: to win. In the game of tag, your goal if you are "IT" is to touch someone else so you are no longer "IT". The goal for players who aren't "IT" is to run away from the person who is to avoid getting tagged. Players tend to make rules such as the boundaries of where the game is contained, how high the "IT" needs to count while the others are moving away, and how the game actually ends. Every person who plays the game is influenced by how they want to play based on their own previous experiences and their personalities. This example shares a basic premise when it comes to games: those involved in the game are not only concerned about the start and end of the game, but the PROCESS needed to move through the game experience.

Let's be clear – it's important to understand that all players involved in the game develop some type of relationship with the rule-maker. In business, that rule maker is YOU, boss lady! You are the ultimate woman in charge in ensuring that your customers receive the optimal experience at every stage in their journey. It's just as important – I would actually state MORE important – to make sure your employees feel or experience the following:

- appreciated,
- an equitable environment
- meaningful work
- opportunities for growth and development,
- effective communication,
- personally healthy,
- the company is healthy,
- safe
- business and personal visions align.

Jane McGonigal is the Director of Game Research at Institute for the Future, and her vision is incredible about where games can take us – look up her TED talks, interviews, articles, and books. She succinctly summarizes the employee feelings above when stating, "Games are explicitly designed to improve quality of life, to prevent suffering, and to create real, widespread happiness." What happens if these items are not addressed? The employee metrics will most likely not be met. Worse, you may lose good employees! If you've heard of the Great Resignation[2] of 2021 and the Great Reshuffle[3] of 2021, then you understand what I mean. A thriving business can occur when you purposely address the employee experience. If the employee experience suffers, so can

[2] The Great Resignation is the moniker given the mass exodus of employees who voluntarily quit their employment. According to U.S Bureau of Labor Statistic JOLTS report, 4.4 million workers quit in September, 2021. A driving factor for this trend is that employees were dissatisfied with the working conditions or pay that
[3] The Great Reshuffle emerged from the Great Resignation. People were moving from jobs that they did not like (for various reasons) to jobs they felt gave them the right pay, work arrangements, and benefits., This was especially noted in employees with skills in high-demand industries.

the customer experience which can be measured by NPS scores, negative social media posts, and/or decreased revenue. Make no mistake: Your business lives or dies by your leadership.

Recognize that both employees and customers take a journey that you create. Choosing inaction is actually a choice – and making the choice to not craft a plan can sabotage your future success. You must develop creative strategies to positively impact your employees directly through processes put into place to help them do their jobs. And just in case you forgot, let me remind you:

Everyone has creativity within them. It's just a matter of unlocking that creativity.

**~ Christina Canters,
Founder and CEO,** *The C Method*

You also must strategize what your customers should experience when in contact with your business, whether they are in contact with you directly or your employees. In addition to the goal you have for your clients or employees, one particular goal is often not addressed -- that is to have some fun along this journey! This is where incorporating gamification strategies can help.

BUSINESS METRICS: What You Treasure, Measure

Metrics and KPIs are often used interchangeably. You and your project teams are identifying the impact a proposed project has from the various stakeholder perspectives; ensure data from the perspectives are being captured. A word of advice – *don't overkill with data.* Once you find metrics that work for the project, stick with them. Measure beyond individual points-in-time to identify trends when possible. Continue encouraging your teams as they create the project, and celebrate with them in embracing their creativity whether the initial goal was achieved or not. When you incorporate your game strategies, you want to align them with your business metrics.

GAMIPHI, the Customer Journey

The customer journey refers to the path of interactions the customer has with your brand while the employee journey is the entire time they spend interacting with the company. The plan you create based on the customer or employee journey is called the journey map, which is a visual representation of the experience. Neither the customer nor employee journey is based on an isolated event; rather, it focuses on the complete sum of the connection with your business. I'm not coming to you from a marketer's perspective, but instead as a small business owner perspective so you can develop a plan to use gamification to enhance these experiences.

Customer-focused Game Plan

Listen – I know you are in your business because you have a purpose, goals, and a mission you want to fulfill, and you bring your own special sauce that you just KNOW will help your customers. We've all been there. You've tried the suggestions that others have shared to help make your business pop including a comprehensive content marketing strategy and buying ads. And those measures absolutely work, but we're also embracing another strategic tool that keeps your customer present by using games that take her from a prospect to a brand ambassador. We want her shouting praises about your products and/or services to anyone and everyone who will listen.

Customers have the ability to influence the decisions of your small business. They have a vast amount of knowledge about certain products, equipping them with the strength to discern and choose between similar products. For this reason, a customer journey map is needed. A customer journey map is a tool that is used to physically identify how much interaction and engagement a customer has with your product or service to help you create a better customer experience. What I want to challenge you with is taking the customer journey just a little bit further and gamifying it. Make it more engaging, via messages and other forms of interaction, without necessarily going out of your way to incur costs trying to pay them a visit. You also get to save the time you would have otherwise spent in front of your counter, trying to coax an honest opinion of your brand out of your customer. Let's briefly review the four states of a buyer's journey: awareness, consideration, decision-making/conversion, and support.

Awareness

When a potential customer first learns about your product or service, they're at the beginning of awareness. By using automated and gamified marketing techniques, you learn what topics most interest your prospective client to better serve them information they can use. You build a higher level of awareness that leads to more engagement with your brand, and, most importantly, sets your business apart from similar brands, thereby creating a niche in the market for you.

Consideration

Once you have your customer's attention and present products or services that fulfill a need, they consider doing business with you. How you serve them the answer to their problem provides you with the data about additional solutions you can offer.

Conversion/Purchase

Your customer is ready to purchase, and excellent customer service is critical even if you don't have direct contact with your buyer. Collecting their information and ensuring efficient (fast) delivery should feel effortless on their part, and if there is an issue, you absolutely need standard operating procedures in place to address it.

Support

When your loyal customers become your business advocates, you've gained the support that closes the customer journey circle. Support takes many forms; positive reviews, telling family and friends, creating unboxing videos for their own social media accounts, becoming an affiliate, and more.

Every stage of your customer's journey has the potential to incorporate gamification.

Sandra Cleveland, Ph.D., RN

EXAMPLE:
"GAMIPHI" TO SEGMENT YOUR TARGET AUDIENCE

Scenario: One of the big tasks you will be doing with your audience is marketing to them. While I could search out and provide a more robust definition of marketing, know that it really comes down to the premise of you making your customers interested in your company's services and products. We need to first know who the target customers are.

There are three steps that need to be completed to find your target audience:

1. Identify the layers of your customers.
2. Verify your audience with a trusted partner.
3. Create a quick survey for some of your audience.

You need to have it at the back of your mind that everyone cannot be your target audience. There are various questions that when answered properly can give you a vivid understanding of your customers. Once you have identified the target audience, you may find that this audience can be further subdivided into smaller groups that you can market more specifically. This idea is called segmented marketing. Some questions to be asked may include: Who are your customers going to be? What is the situation that each subgroup of customers is currently in? Where is the current location of your customers? Gamifying some of the marketing strategies can be used to help obtain answers to these questions because, in addition to or creation of a profile by customers in order to use platforms to purchase goods and services, customers provide the basic needed information or can give out such information while doing business.

How might you use gamification to segment the individuals who are actually your audience? Getting to know your clients and their taste can be provided easily, which on a normal small business without gamification is more difficult to obtain.

Let's take an example. When you have a potential customer sign up for a free offering such as joining your newsletter or community, a welcome email is a great way to welcome them to your tribe. But you can up the ante! What if you developed a welcome email with a gamified twist as a way to begin a journey with your clients when first-time subscribers purchase a product or service? Through use of automation, the act of purchase by your customer will trigger a welcome email to appear on their screens. Then through the use of gamification, you can engage your customer to not only get the free offering to them but have them play a decision-making game such as "this-or-that", allowing them to choose their preferences. This makes a memorable impression on them and can give you valuable data in tweaking your offering based on the business marketing metrics.

CHAPTER 4
GAMIFICATION
FOR HAPPIER EMPLOYEES

Employee-focused Game Plan

Have you ever just sat and thought about how many ways your potential or active employees have made contact with your brand? It's not only how individual employees directly serve the customer. The employee journey also consists of the touchpoints where the employee is developing personally and professionally through the organization. Your organizational culture is expressed in how you reach out to individuals to make them aware of job openings, even those with stretch goals. It's also demonstrated by the ways you get an employee acclimated to the organization's culture.

If you are not making the effort to plan your employees' journey, they absolutely will jump ship for a job that better meets their needs. The proof is in the tight job market of 2022:

- According to the Job Openings and Labor Turnover Survey (JOLTS), the "Great Resignation" in the United States saw a record 4.53 million workers quit their jobs in March 2022.
- Half of the people who left their job switched their field of work – bringing on what was called the "Great Reshuffle".
- It costs CEOs approximately 1.5 to 2 times the amount of pay to replace a worker who leaves.

Your business operations and processes help establish and inform the organizational culture. Although formal operations and processes do help your employees navigate their roles, these alone do not make your employees want to stay. The employee who feels valued is more likely to not just stay at the company, but actively engage. If employees actively stay engaged, productivity, morale, and profits improve. Data supports this point. The 2021 Gallup Poll shared that companies with engaged employees make 2.5x more revenue!

From the moment you begin onboarding a new team member until that employee resigns, everything he or she goes through while still a paid member of your business forms the employee journey. A journey map is needed to help the Human Resource team (which is most likely YOU) apportion tasks and operations and understand where your employee experience needs attention.

The journey map further enables your small business to prioritize the particular moments that matter to the growth of the employee, like their emotional state and monthly pay, by physically drawing out each stage, and making sufficient plans for engagement and productivity. An employee journey map brings to light the unnoticed experiences of each employee, the particular talent niche of an employee, and identifies the much-needed avenue to promote equality and full participation. This, in turn, leads to a higher level of effectiveness and productivity.

Four key areas of consideration in the journey map are recruitment and onboarding, development, recognition and evaluation, retainment, and offboarding.

Recruitment and Onboarding

You've heard the adage, "If you build it, they will come". As Girl Bosses, we know this is not often the case! You can't just depend on hopes, dreams, and prayers that the ideal employee will come your way. You have to make the presence of your business known to the right audiences. You have to then put a plan in place to help them find you.

Your small business will remain invisible to prospective employees if awareness is not created for the targeted labor force. Employee awareness and onboarding are some of the most important connections an employer has with her employees. The creation of an efficient onboarding process is bound to attract the right employees, and create the best impressions. The awareness and onboarding of an applicant implies taking the necessary steps in ensuring that newly hired employees have substantial knowledge of your business's mission and vision, their specific duties as well as an introduction into the resources needed for the successful completion of their tasks.

When you develop your organizational culture using strategic gamification, you are recognized as a thought leader who embraces the employee experience from the moment they find you! This whole process ensures that newly hired employees are properly empowered for their jobs and constantly acts as a reminder for why they accepted the job. There is a plethora of simple online software that helps with employee onboarding checklists, creating a smooth transition from applicant to team member and further reducing the potential for costly turnover.

EXAMPLE:
GAMIFY RECRUITMENT AND ONBOARDING

Pokémon GO was a big game a few years ago. Kids in your life were probably playing this game. Heck, adults played just as much as the kids! Pokémon GO is a mobile app that combines augmented reality within a real-world environment, and it was utterly amazing! Players were tasked with finding Pokémon characters and then fighting them, but many players had fun just participating in the search for the characters. This game was essentially a scavenger hunt.

A scavenger hunt is a great way to introduce potential applicants to your small business. Long gone are the days when the applicant had to just read manuals and forms and have minimal interaction with other employees. Your scavenger hunt can incorporate a social aspect by including current employees and you, too, along the journey.

Before you bring anyone new onboard, use a scavenger hunt to take them through your website. Introduce them to your mission, vision, and values—whatever you want them to learn about.

Once the applicant becomes a team member, take them through another scavenger hunt designed to help them get acclimated to your company. Start building this by incorporating your current onboarding checklist and include the completion of necessary forms. Take it to the next level by creating a storyline within the scavenger hunt and include the necessity of interacting with their colleagues. Incentivize completing goals your new employee encounters throughout their onboarding process.

EXAMPLE:
"GAMIPHI" a TEAM MEETING

Scenario: Employee productivity is largely dependent on their connection to each other and their ability to work together as a team. The evolution of every modern workplace ensures that employees can now remain employed and carry out tasks without their actual location being taken into consideration. A lot of tools and applications have been created to build on the different forms of communication. There are tons of productive business tools making teamwork easier from any location in the world. There are online video conferencing tools that make formal meetings possible without the stress of leaving your home and spending on transportation. It also eliminates the possible excuses that might arise as to why an employee is unable to make it to a physical conference.

While having a number of meeting tools is definitely a step in the right direction, many business owners struggle with getting their teams truly involved in the meetings. But WE are NOT other business owners! We need to take engagement up a notch, Girl Boss. Gamification strategies can facilitate brainstorming on critical decisions needed to be taken in your business.

There are a few items that you need to consider before moving forward with the exercise. I will add these reminder questions again for other examples:

What is the goal of the activity in general?

Who is going to benefit from the activity?

How did you assess the situation?

What *output* KPIs might be developed based on this situation?

What *input* KPIs might be developed based on this situation?

What will you use to measure the effectiveness of the activity?

One example is combining the ideas of gamification with storytelling in your team meeting. I call this gamified meeting example "SLAY the DRAGON," which could be used for projects that will entail multiple team meetings:

Whoever is the project lead can make up and share the background story of the dragon. There are sub teams designated, who tell stories about how the dragon has impacted their particular kingdom. Each team creates a character representative of them to act in the game. In this meeting format, you award points and badging. Points can be based on participation while badges are gained at key points on the quest to slay the dragon.

Individuals on each team have the ability to "power up" and gain individual points, which can be used towards a prize. The "power up" occurs when their character goes to the other kingdoms to present an idea and those kingdoms are willing to incorporate it. Teams can earn badges, which might be redeemed for a team prize. Health and fun mini-missions can be built across the kingdom (and can be viewed or hidden). They can be completed and proof shared for health/fun related prizes.

Employee Recognition and Evaluation

Feedback and reviews serve as a very important means of identifying the strengths and areas of improvement of your employees, which provides an avenue for growth. The success of your business is a huge reflection of the performance level of your employees. It is important they receive recognition for a job well done in order to make them feel appreciated and satisfied and they understand why they did not receive an anticipated promotion or salary raise. The evaluation process doesn't guarantee your workers are fulfilled, of course. An automated employee recognition award system can help you manage this possible incentive.

EXAMPLE:
GAMIFY EMPLOYEE RECOGNITION AND EVALUATION

Ms. SHE-EO, you need to make your appreciation of your employees' work known. The lack of recognition and consistent evaluation leaves employees unsure and contributes to worker turnover. This means that you have to move beyond the old standards such as annual evaluations to find ways to meet employees where they are at.

The Amazing Race was an American television show that ran for many years where teams of two people competed against up to 12 other teams tasked with navigating through different legs of a journey through a number of countries to reach an ultimate destination. Prizes were awarded not only for the ultimate winner but also at different legs of the game as well based on teams successfully completing challenges along the way. The host of the game shared the leaderboard so that teams knew where they were in the rankings. Use this game as the premise to create your own amazing race! Your amazing race can be set up in a live or virtual environment and must include a definitive end goal as well as a series of smaller goals workers will encounter along the way. Once you've identified the smaller goals, break them down further by identifying skills you want employees to attain during the game. For instance, employees working in teams builds their ability to work as part of a team.

The next portion of creating your amazing race is to identify how you can recognize employees during the journey and once the race is completed. In addition to earning points for meeting benchmarks and finishing the game, give employees the opportunity to choose how they can use their points. Employees receive reward and recognition both internally and externally, so giving them some control over how they spend their "prize money" goes a long way.

Create a shop where employees can spend their points. For instance, you might have three categories of prizes:

- Products they can buy;
- Things/activities for wellness, personal development (think days off or courses they want to attend); and
- Philanthropic causes they can support.

You can give your workers even more autonomy by allowing them to choose how they allocate their points. For example, they can dedicate percentages of points to categorizes of prizes:

- Prizes they can buy: 50%
- Prizes for wellness, personal development: 40%
- Philanthropic causes they can support: 10%

See what you just did here, Ms. CEO? You provided a recognition strategy that empowers your employees – making it more meaningful for them to want to complete the race. Now, you're probably thinking there's no way you can afford three categories of prizes for your employees. First, you don't have to do everything yourself. Second, identify your budget. Third, contact a company that supports employee reward systems and choose one that meets your budget. Do you see how we tackled employee recognition? Additional ideas could include providing feedback at each benchmark; having your employees complete a journal that chronicles their experience with the game, and incorporating a leaderboard for all teams, not just the top teams, can be a motivating factor as well because it introduces a level of competition. Just make sure you watch your employees to see if the competition keeps attitudes positive or creates stress. Can you see the possibilities?

Gamification provides meaningful rewards for employee contributions at the same time you share appreciation for them. Gamification can also be used to design evaluations providing meaningful, timely feedback to encourage desired behaviors or to move toward these behaviors. Remember, this is about engaging your employees throughout their tenure with your business.

Employee Development

Creating a positive work culture entails a deeply rooted interest in the employees. Let me state this again for the back of the room: As CEO, you must move beyond perfunctory efforts so your employees know, like, and trust you. Sound familiar? Employee engagement is their commitment and devotion for and toward your business's mission, you, and fellow employees, which increases their productivity and performance. In 2020, Korn Ferry conducted a study to compare the engagement level of a set of employees and the resulting generated revenue: their most engaged offices reported   an average of $72,000 more than the least engaged ones.

Where does gamification come into play for employee development? Think about employees who may be sitting on the proverbial sideline because they want to engage in something meaningful, but aren't sure if they would be accepted. Another example are those employees who appear bored – not because they are not capable, but because they aren't being used in a capacity that is fulfilling to them and can help meet the organization's objectives at the same time. You can gamify opportunities in order for your employees to find ways to become a real part of the organization, such as gaining skills for leadership succession.

EXAMPLE:
GAMIFY EMPLOYEE DEVELOPMENT

"Success is getting what you see on the inside to manifest on the outside."

~ T.D. Jakes

Personal and professional development is at the crux of maintaining a strong relationship with your employees. It's essentially a promise that you are going to offer real value for their professional and personal lives in exchange for them giving their best to your company. You want to provide an employee development strategy that allows employees to have flexibility, maintain a good work-life balance, and explore growth and advancement opportunities. The advantages of offering employee development from your perspective:

- Provides your business a competitive edge
- Increases employee motivation
- Increases employee engagement

I call this gamification strategy "The Shape Shifter". A shape shifter is an imaginary being who can change their physical shape. For the purpose of employee development, I extend the definition to include changes to their mind and spirit. Employees choose their adventures, working through a series of courses in order to shape shift to their new form. NOTE: Your courses can also use gamified strategies as well.

Badges can be used as part of the reward strategy, so get creative with the badges. For instance, I might ask them to develop an avatar of what they will look like once they shape shift. The avatar can then be broken apart for different badges and put back together once the employee successfully completes the series of courses they chose. The beautiful thing about this strategy is that employees may choose to shape shift again and again based on new goals they develop during their tenure with you. SHE-EO, one of the biggest takeaways about employee development is that your employee needs to have ownership of their journey, to determine what personal and professional development activities they'll complete. Your role is to help them build – whether it's acquiring new skills to work on a project beyond their current job description or to be promoted. Used strategically, gamification is one tool in your arsenal you provide to accomplish this.

Retain

There are things that you, Ms. SHE-EO, need to understand from the employee's perspective. These items do not necessarily fall under employee development but impact workplace productivity. Have you ever been in a job where a survey was taken about the employees' needs? The employer reaches out repeatedly to have the survey completed. But once the survey has been completed you never hear about it again. What happened to it? In this example, the employer dropped the ball. The workers may have pointed out poor processes, lack of communication among departments, or other concerns that present opportunities the employer should have addressed. Unfortunately, the lack of communication from the employer on the survey results and the lack of subsequent action steps may result in workers feeling unheard and frustrated about performing to the best of their ability.

In the brief description of the GamiPHI Theory shared earlier, we learned the considerations small business owners must address in the employee experience that can impact productivity. Your employees are making decisions every day on whether they stay or leave your organization based on the personal checks and balances they identify. These checks-and-balances include their perception of the environmental, innovative potential, and personal and organizational health. If these considerations are not addressed, your employees can check out even when they are on the clock—presenteeism—choose not to engage, and even leave. Retaining your employees not only in the organization but in the right role within the organization matters.

Offboard

There are many different reasons why an employee may part ways with your business. According to Gallup, "Leaving the organization can be the most emotional and uncertain phase of an employee's journey. When employees have a positive exit experience, they're more likely to become proud brand ambassadors who strengthen your brand's reputation." Small business owners need to understand the reason an employee leaves. For instance, if the employee says she was bored in her role, was there a way that you could have helped her upskill towards another role within your organization? Ideally, you should be holding conversations with your employees throughout their tenure at the organization to gauge opportunities where you can intervene before it gets to this point. Please understand that employees will move on for various reasons so you cannot take it personally. However, you can develop a clearer understanding of why they are leaving, and how you can help prevent future employees from doing the same.

The way a company treats its individuals never goes unnoticed. Professionals are constantly and silently evaluating whether their boss' qualities line up with their own, and making decisions based on these perceptions. As a result of the employee experience map, employee loyalty to your brand is identified, and you demonstrate your commitment to your employees. Companies need to start positioning both the employee and the processes in ways that allow for growth and adaptability.

It's not solely about the end goals.

The way in which we get work done must make sense to the needs of the employees. Furthermore, this awareness can't be overlooked when it comes to virtual spaces. When virtual interactions are treated as though only the end goal matters, employees notice, and it sends a message that the process, their time, and their experience don't matter. We need to be deft and ready to reset needs or pull together groups on a more standard foundation.

CHAPTER 5
LET THE GAMES BEGIN!

G ood job, Ms. CEO! You've identified strategies to organize your business processes so that you do not have to be in the business of your business. The next step is building gamification strategies into the customer and employee experiences. If I have not convinced you quite yet about how gamification can be, well, a game-changer for your business, let me share a couple of additional stats stated in Finances Online:

* 89% of U.S. workers report that workplace gamification would make them more productive
* 80% of U.S. workers find gamification-based learning more engaging than traditional training

Leaders in multiple industries have incorporated gamification into their strategies for their employees in many areas of the business. Here are additional examples I found on Finances Online:

- ❖ M&M's created a gaming app, Eye Spy Pretzel, which helped the brand rack up 25,000 new Facebook likes and 6,000 shares.
- ❖ Duolingo, which leverages gamification in teaching languages to users for free via mobile, has grown its user base to over 300 million.
- ❖ LivingSocial decided to turn its annual reviews into gamified experiences, which resulted in more than 90% voluntarily participating.
- ❖ In a report by Ohio University in 2020, they found that Target created an app through which users can create Christmas wish lists, which generated 75,000 initial downloads. During the holiday season, the app amassed over 100,000 wish lists, 1.7 million entered items, and sales of $92.3 million.

Just to be clear, these statistics apply to employees of different demographics such as age and gender. Don't stop gamification in your organization because of predetermined standards on what a 'gamer' looks like.

Take heart. The fact that you and other Girl Bosses are reading this book and applying gamification into your business shows that there are other "gamers" like you! You have an amazing opportunity to share your expertise as a subject matter expert with other SHE-EOs and develop a membership of like-minded individuals.

Strategy Example #1: Build and Monetize your own Girl Boss Mastermind Group

It's no secret that you can go a lot further with others than you can on your own. When you're by yourself, you're limited by your own knowledge and experience. When things get tough, it is easy to get discouraged and want to give up. It can be difficult to stay motivated over the long haul. You can benefit from the insights and hard-won experience of others. When you're feeling frustrated or burned out, they can encourage you and help you keep going. If your motivation is flagging, they can push you.

Albert Schweitzer said: In everyone's life, at some time, our inner fire goes out. It is then burst into flame by an encounter with another human being. We should all be thankful for those people who rekindle the inner spirit.

Of course, this raises the question: how can you surround yourself with others who will help you be your best self? How can you connect with those who will rekindle your inner creative spirit? An option is to be the subject matter expert in a SHE-EO mastermind group that YOU create and invite other Girl Bosses to join you. What is a mastermind group? A mastermind group is a collection of like-minded people who are pursuing similar goals and objectives.

Notice, there are two elements to a mastermind group. First, it's a collection of like-minded individuals. One caveat – be careful of using your definition of "like-minded" – expand the definition to incorporate diverse thoughts to encourage creative idea expansion. This does not mean that everyone thinks the same way. It does not mean there isn't disagreement. It simply means that everyone is headed in essentially the same direction. Second, everyone in the group is pursuing similar goals and objectives. Because everyone is going after the same thing, they can encourage and help each other along the way.

All members of the group:

- Share insights and knowledge. You benefit from the combined years of experience and deep knowledge of all the members of your group. They can provide you with insights that can only be gained in the trenches.
- Give encouragement. There will be times when you don't feel like continuing to push forward. In these tired, discouraging moments, the members of your mastermind can give you very specific encouragement because they know what you're going through.
- Help each other navigate challenges. In moments of confusion or difficulty, mastermind members can take you by the hand. They can give you suggestions and tips you would never think of yourself.
- Provide resources. You have the opportunity to share and receive valuable resources, such as books, articles, videos, and podcasts.
- Hold each other accountable. Having others hold you accountable for your goals ensures that you keep making forward progress. Knowing that you're going to be regularly updating them on how things are going can help you stay motivated over the long run.

Girl, Get in the Game!

Napoleon Hill, author of the book *Think and Grow Rich*, described mastermind groups like this:

The coordination of knowledge and effort of two or more people, who work toward a definite purpose, in the spirit of harmony; no two minds ever come together without thereby creating a third, invisible intangible force, which may be likened to a third mind.

Mastermind groups aren't a new concept. Business titans Andrew Carnegie and Henry Ford were part of masterminds. Oprah Winfrey effectively described the purpose of masterminds when she said, "Surround yourself with people who are going to lift you higher."

When choosing who's in your mastermind, seek out individuals who are growth minded. Anthony Iannarino puts it this way:

It's essential that you find people who are growth-oriented for a mastermind. The people in your mastermind must be driven to be more, do more, have more, and contribute more (my shorthand for striving to reach your full potential). It isn't enough that they want the camaraderie alone. They need to bring something to the table. You can't build an effective mastermind with people who aren't striving, or who are merely drifting.

The bottom line is that you want to invite Girl Bosses who can do two things: add and receive value.

What is the benefit of you developing your own Girl Boss

mastermind?

Girl, you come into this with a wealth of knowledge and skills that other Girl Bosses would love to obtain. You often hear that knowledge is power. In this age of digital information, knowledge is a thought commodity. In other words – other CEOs are waiting and willing to pay for access to information you're willing to provide and help them apply. Women CEOs are living proof that we can make a way out of no way! Think about the ways you obtained funding, employees, and customers for your business. My guess is that you had to find alternate strategies to get it done. Your ability to innovate extends to delivering your content in new ways! I believe that YOU can build a mastermind based on new and innovative ways to convey information to fellow SHE-EOs, to assess their learning, and to provide feedback. Your mastermind is also another stream of revenue for your business. How can you monetize your Girl Boss mastermind?

You can identify various ways for the SHE-EOs to pay for your mastermind but one of the ways that might be effective for you is to charge based on the value of the information you are sharing and applying the information. In setting your price, ask yourself: what would make my mastermind worth it to my fellow Girl Bosses? For instance, if the SHE-EOS invest in your mastermind for $20,000 and make an additional $150,000 from the information you provided, then they would deem it a good investment. To develop your fee structure, first start by identifying the costs associated with running the group (i.e., administrative, team member pay, marketing, etc.) and then choose a price (and please, please do not underestimate your worth, Ma'am).

"GAMIPHI" Your Mastermind Members' Skills

You may have SHEEOs who have the drive and desire to want to be involved, but you are struggling with the notion that they may lack needed knowledge or skills. What can you do? Girl, you are a thought-leader. You know based on the GAMIPHI Theory that gamification can be used for knowledge and skill development. This development doesn't have to be attached only to expected areas in the employee's journey. This is also used for leadership development. One way to do this is to help your potential mastermind members *job craft* through gamification. Let me explain: Job crafting is the idea that leaders can proactively transform their work experience without having to change careers or even search for a new position. Organizational behaviorists started talking about job crafting 20 or so years ago. Reviewing each CEO's job description and daily activities is usually the first step.

You would need to identify the knowledge and skills needed to become an effective mastermind member. You can develop a suite of small games designed to build those skills effectively (make sure to label the gained skills in the game's description). The potential mastermind members can then complete those games and submit proof of completion to be considered. Those who don't complete their self-selected games may not be ready yet – and that's okay! You may work with those individuals to find their interests and better align with their current job role.

Strategy Example #2: Evaluate the Effectiveness of Activities Towards Your Goal

Remember my SLAY THE DRAGON meeting example that I shared earlier? It was based on a way to "gamiphi" your meetings. You might create a mastermind group who can help your meetings evolve into something truly effective. But how will you know if it is effective? One, you will have first determined the metric(s) so there's a clear understanding of the outcomes. Two, you will develop the assessment tools that will be used to measure the metrics.

Every few months, it will be helpful to step back and evaluate how things are going. This allows you to make necessary adjustments, get feedback from the members, and ensure that everyone is getting maximum value from the group.

Some things to consider when you evaluate are:

- Personal objectives. Overall, do you feel like the mastermind is helping you achieve what you desire? If not, what needs to change?
- Project objectives. How well are you meeting the group objectives towards the project? Take the opportunity to survey members about their impressions.
- Member feedback. What things would the members like to change? What do they like? What do they dislike?
- Size. Is the group a good size? Would it become more effective by adding more members or splitting into smaller groups?

- Format. Is the current format working well? Are the meetings too short or long? Is everyone able to participate equally? Would a different format work better?

Based on the answers to the above questions, you can make changes and improvements to your mastermind group goals. It's important, however, that you don't make changes unilaterally. In other words, don't change things without first consulting the group. This has the potential to offend people and create division. Ensure that everyone is on board before you alter things. It can also be helpful to give the members a chance to leave the group. Not everyone will want to stay in the group indefinitely. Some may benefit most from just a few months with the group. Some may experience a schedule change. Give members the opportunity to leave without any hard feelings. You want to preserve the valuable relationships you've built within the group.

How Can We GAMIPHI Evaluation in Masterminds?

Your mastermind group members each have goals for their businesses. They should also have goals for themselves. Goals don't mean anything if they are not evaluated for the effectiveness of actions put into place to achieve them. Just like for our employees, SHE-EOs don't want to deal with a bunch of mundane activities. Here are things to consider when developing the evaluation techniques for evaluation.

Use the reminder questions first:

- What is the goal of the activity in general?
- Who is going to benefit from the activity?
- How did you assess the situation?
- What *output* KPIs might be developed based on this situation?
- What *input* KPIs might be developed based on this situation?
- What will you use to measure the effectiveness of the activity?

EXAMPLE: THE PUZZLE

In the case study, there were six main goals. If masterminds were created for each goal, then each mastermind would be responsible for the achievement of the milestone goals, personal goals, meeting goals, and other metrics. Create a BIG, virtual (or portable) puzzle board – each puzzle piece represents a goal that each group member wants to achieve in addition to the project milestones. You could also have each group member identify a goal in categories such as, "A soft skill I want to learn," "A task I want to lead," or whatever the group chooses.

Here's the fun – surprise them and add a group prize behind the puzzle pieces! As the goals are achieved, the team members remove those puzzle pieces, revealing the group prize. If goals are met in the specified time frame, then the prize will be awarded to the group.

Strategy Example #3: GamiPHI SHEEO Recognition in Masterminds

SHEEO – you work hard to recognize others in the industry and in your business, but too often you don't receive recognition for the challenges faced in your role. Recognition is often one of the biggest struggles organizations face because one form of recognition may work for one leader but fails completely for another. Gamification can be used to help address this. You want to recognize your mastermind members not just when a task is completed, but in the completion of milestones towards that task as well.

Let me share an example that is not CEO related, but captures this idea. Like many parents, I struggled getting my kids motivated to do their chores. I'd suggest, beg, cajole, and threaten. There are companies out there that recognize this is an issue for a lot of parents, and they developed apps with gaming features to incentivize chores (it's like gig services directed towards kids). Here is how it works:

- Parents identify the chores and the pay associated with them.
- Kids check off completed chores in the app and receive immediate payment.
- Kids watch their money grow.
- Parents can help their kids become financially savvy.

Sandra Cleveland, Ph.D., RN

How Do You "GamiPHI" Incentivizing the Girl Bosses in Your Mastermind?

You should provide options based on both personal and professional development goals that will ultimately meet the needs of your members' organizations. I know you may wonder how personal goals fit into your business's success. Let's take an example based on health and fitness.

Losing weight is usually one of the three biggest New Year's resolutions people make but rarely achieve. One of the reasons they fail is the inability to incorporate new and healthier habits within the work environment. SHE-EOs typically spend a third to almost half of their waking hours at work. Let's review our reminder questions again for this scenario:

- What is the goal of the activity in general?
- Who is going to benefit from the activity?
- How did you assess the situation?
- What *output* KPIs might be developed based on this situation?
- What *input* KPIs might be developed based on this situation?
- What will you use to measure the effectiveness of the activity?

You might create a group weight loss competition that is based not strictly on weight loss, but other measures of health such as adding more fruits and vegetables, getting more sleep, and fun. Yes, fun is allowed at work and in your mastermind! You can create a virtual leaderboard to monitor everyone's progress. Find apps out there that focus on meeting the desired health outcomes, and select one that best fits your needs. The contest would focus on team and individual milestones.

I hope with the three examples I've shared that your brain is starting to see the possibilities of what GamiPHI can add initially to your mastermind group and later to your organization. Although the examples I shared are targeting SHE-EOs, you can apply these concepts to the customer and employee experience as well. There are many ways, both small and large, you can positively impact your organization's people and processes to make an even more positive impact on your customers and your revenue. Adding gamification can make the environment more playful, healthier, and more innovative as a result.

Ladies, have you heard the following quote?

Women must learn to play the game as men do.

~ Eleanor Roosevelt

Now, our girl, Eleanor, was a badass lady – and based on her experiences and those of many other women – I agree with the sentiment. However, I hope that this book shows that women not only learned to play the games to acclimate into a man's world, but we now create our own games.

We must use gamification to build our businesses and *REDEFINE THE GAME*.

A FINAL NOTE: "K.I.S.S.ES"

A s you read through this book, you hopefully started thinking about how much you can do with your organization, but where do you start? One of the best pieces of advice that I share is K.I.S.S.(es) – that's right – there are two kisses that are important to remember.

The first kiss: Keep It Simple and Sane. For instance, you may look at your HR metrics and determine that a couple of infrastructure changes need to be made for stronger recognition of psychological safety within the organization – that's a great goal. But how do you move it from an idea to an actionable initiative? Present the idea to internal stakeholders and let them help decide which initiatives you'll move forward. You, as the leader, have to ensure how psychological safety is going to be evident in this project as an example. Use brainstorming sessions to determine what might be done, then allow stakeholders to pick ONE item they feel they can creatively pursue. Recognize that using gamification and playing can be used for the brainstorming sessions. And the brainstorming need not be limited to the work – incorporate play as well.

The second kiss: Keep It Simple and Sustainable. Remember, your ultimate goal when incorporating gamification is to improve the customer and your employee experiences. The types of gamifications that you incorporate might be refined – that's okay. But the concept of GAMIPHI is a technique that can be woven into your strategies for years to come.

Minimizing the extraneous effort
can help maximize the impact towards the desired project.

Don't forget to celebrate the unconventional critical and creative thinking individuals across the organization who identified the issues and moved the project forward. Please do not wait until project completion! Recognition for meeting project milestones as well as the individual and group creativity need to be celebrated throughout the journey as well. Just as important: celebrate the attempts. Every project is not going to run smoothly, and attempts may not succeed. Highlighting the efforts in the quest for a healthy creative small business is just as (if not more) important for company growth to occur. This differentiates the small businesses who embrace players versus those whose players disengage and move to the sidelines.

Celebrate the gamers as well! These are the individuals tasked with transforming the organization one group or unit at a time. Effective leadership is essential for driving creativity and innovation, effective employee and customer care and safety, improving work within teams, and other aspects necessary for the effective and efficient running of the organization. Celebrate leaders who take efforts to move beyond transactional leadership (based on reward for performance) to transformational leadership.

Finally, celebrate YOU!

Ms. SHE-EO, you are truly phenomenal. In the midst of competing circumstances such as family, school, and a little pandemic, you are running a business. YOUR BUSINESS. Allow yourself to celebrate the small and big things that come along during this journey.

Girl, you ready? Get in the Game!

ACKNOWLEDGEMENTS

Always first and foremost is my Heavenly Father.

For my anchor of ancestors who allow me to get to this stage…

My parents – my original earthly faith-builders…

To present people in my life who have crossed paths for a reason, season, or lifetime…

To my futures who always remind me that hope is key…

Thank you for the gift of YOU.

Finally, to my fellow SHEEOs…continue to Make It Happen!

Cephus, Lena & Lavalle - Thank you for believing in me and allowing me to pursue my dream of becoming an author who helps others pursue their dreams. Without your never-ending support, this would not have been possible.

Dad and Mom (AKA James and Geria Fleming, AKA the parental units) – I need to write a book by itself just to thank you two for everything you have done and sacrificed so that I had options. I absolutely love, adore, and appreciate you.

Sandra Cleveland, Ph.D., RN

To Charron Monaye and her team at Pen Legacy Publishing. Charron, the person you are and the services that you provide are unparalleled. Thank you for all the insight, encouragement, 'gentle reminders,' and silence at the right times. Tamika Hall – the book cover is amazing! Karen Langley, thank you for being the hub and keeping us organized.

To my editor, Heather Asiyanbi, who totally understood the assignment from day one. A rough draft was never so rough!! You challenged me to redevelop the ideas. Never was I so thankful as when you broke down the rough draft so we could rebuild it better. You encouraged me to find my true voice and I am forever grateful. You are phenomenal at what you do.

Finally, to my sounding boards who listened to me share (and reshare) my vision for the message at different stages along this journey: Alvionna Brewster, Dr. Sandra Curtis, Elle Pierson, Michelle Greene Rhodes, Dr. Viola Pierce, Myown Holmes, Jameisha Rogers, and Stephanie Freeman.

And finally, my sister-circle who were there for me and allowed me to just *be*: my Auntie/Sis Laynora Hill-King, Jill Hoegemeyer Bettendorf, Rana Cleveland, Tabitha Denard, Debra Wheeler, Tracey Cleveland-Halleck, and Yvette Forris. Thank you.

References

Chapter 1

Zippia.com (2020). Gamification statistics. https://www.zippia.com/advice/gamification-statistics/

PopCap games (2007). Survey finds executives gaming on office time.https://www.gamedeveloper.com/pc/survey-finds-execs-gaming-on-office-time

Pelling, Nick. (Jan 6, 2012). *"The (Short) Prehistory of 'Gamification'..."* *Funding Startups (& Other Impossibilities).* nanodome.wordpress.com/2011/08/09/the-short-prehistory-ofgamification/.

Kapp, K. (2012). *The gamification of learning and instruction: Game-based methods and strategies for training and education (1st ed.).* Pfeiffer.

Chapter 2

Amabile & Mukti Khaire (2008). *Creativity and the role of the leader.* https://hbr.org/2008/10/creativity-and-the-role-of-the-leader.

Pender, N. (2011). Health Promotion Model. https://deepblue.lib.umich.edu/bitstream/handle/2027.42/85350/HEALTH_PROMOTION_MANUAL_Rev_5-2011.pdf

Chapter 4

Job Openings and Labor Turnover Survey, (2022). *The Great Resignation.* U.S. Department of Labor's Bureau of Labor Statistics.

Forbes.com (2022). *The Great Reshuffle.* https://www.forbes.com/sites/jeannemeister/2022/04/19/the-great-re-shuffle-of-talent-what-can-employers-do-to-retain-workers/?sh=77edf2394cf3

Sandra Cleveland, Ph.D., RN

Gallup.com (2019). *This fixable problem costs businesses $1 trillion.*
https://www.gallup.com/workplace/247391/fixable-problem-costs-businesses-trillion.aspx

Korn Ferry (2020). *Future of Engagement.*
https://focus.kornferry.com/employee-engagement/future-of-engagement/

Chapter 5

Finances Online. https://financesonline.com/gamification-statistics/

Ohio University (2020, February 6). Gamification Marketing Examples Being Used in Business. Ohio University

www.ingramcontent.com/pod-product-compliance
Lightning Source LLC
Chambersburg PA
CBHW040907210326
41597CB00029B/4996